Spanish vocabulary for GCSE

In topic categories, with memory techniques

Table of contents

Introduction

Not all students are good at retaining vocabulary. Differences in short and long-term memory skills, together with differing approaches to the stress of learning all go towards making a very uneven playing field when it comes to performance in exams.

I wrote this book to help students remember words without having to spend hours learning lists by heart. As well as setting out the material by topic, I have focused on putting it in context. Equally, I have been realistic about the amount of vocabulary it is possible to learn. There are plenty of books available which will teach you the name of every single animal and every possible computer term but there is little to be gained from overwhelming a student.

One lovely thing about Spanish is the huge number of cognates. I have devoted a whole page to adjectives which are pretty much exactly the same in English and should boost anyone's confidence who struggles with the question: describe your best friend...

Where there isn't a cognate (and Spanish is full of words of Moorish derivation that bear no resemblance to Latin-based or Germanic languages, I have on occasion given you my own strange way of remembering the word. It may not work for you to think that films (peliculas) are all about pelicans, but if it doesn't, and where I haven't provided a memo-technique, you can make up your own.

This book is intended to accompany my previous book in the series "How to Ace your Spanish Oral" and used together these two handbooks will without doubt improve any student's performance in Spanish. In particular, this book will help students enrich and vary their own oral and written answers, allowing them to adapt my answers to suit them.

I wish you all success with your language studies and welcome any feedback you may have via my website

www.lucymartintuition.co.uk

Boosting your confidence with Spanish vocabulary

Before you even start this book, have a read through these pages and remind yourself that a huge number of Spanish words are cognates – ie almost the same as their English equivalents. They fall into various categories:

Words ending in -al in English tend to be the same in Spanish
animal, artificial, brutal, capital, central, criminal, formal, final, general, global, horizontal, hospital, ideal, informal, industrial, legal, local, material, mental, metal, musical, natural, normal, oral, original, personal, regional, sentimental, social, rural, social, universal, verbal, vertical

Other perfect cognates
drama, hotel, horror, terror, invisible, inferior, superior, inevitable, control, idea, error, cancer, chocolate, club, flexible

Words in -tion in English are -ción in Spanish and they are all feminine
reservación, conversación, contaminación, acción, atención, colaboración, clasificación, colección, combinación, concentración, condición, construcción, nación, operación, discriminación, publicación, reacción

Words in -ty in English are -dad and they are all feminine
universidad, sociedad, ciudad (city), calidad (quality), capacidad, comunidad, curiosidad, deformidad, dificultad, cantidad (quantity), velocidad, diversidad, creatividad, celebridad

Words ending in -ic or -ical in English are usually -ico in Spanish
académico, artístico, económico, automático, básico, democrático, clásico, exótico, fantástico, heroico, irónico, mágico, orgánico, plástico, público, romántico, político, psicológico, biológico, físico, cómico

You can also add an o to words ending in ct in English
adicto, conflicto, contacto, correcto, exacto, insecto, perfecto, producto

English words ending in -ous tend to end in -oso in Spanish
religioso, curioso, delicioso, misterioso, tedioso, numeroso, varioso

SO what do these mean?

Un animal brutal

Un error universal

Un club local

Un criminal psicológico

Pizza deliciosa

Una publicación legal

Un problema global

Un hospital básico

Un adicto clásico

Una condición universal

Una idea central

Un producto orgánico

Una capacidad superior

Una sociedad democrática

Una calidad inferior

Una nación perfecta

Una reacción automática

In town

el parque	park
el colegio	school
el supermercado	supermarket
el mercado	market
el centro comercial	shopping centre
el hotel	hotel
el teatro	theatre
el cine	cinema

Words that make sense when you take off the e at the front

estomago	stomach
espinacas	spinach
estudiantes	students
estación	station
estable	stable
estadio	stadium
escándalo	scandal
escenario	scandal
Escocia	Scotland
escuela	school
espacio	space
España	spain
especial	special
espectador	spectator
espinal	spinal
esposo	spouse / husband
esposa	spouse / wife
esquí	skiing
estatua	statue
estrés	stress
estricto	strict
estupendo	amazing (stupendous)

Words that have cognates in French

Don't worry if you don't speak French, but if you do, here is a list of words that you will recognise:

biblioteca	library
fácil	easy
difícil	difficult
malo	bad
mal	badly
bicicleta	bike
jardín	garden
grande	big
enorme	enormous
tranquilo	quiet
simpático	nice
avión	plane
pan	bread
te	tea
fresas	strawberries
frambuesas	raspberries
viejo	old
bien	well
aprender	to learn
el mar	sea
fumar	to smoke
profesor	teacher

There are plenty of other words in Spanish that you will know the meaning of when you hear them.

Read this for example. You'll understand it all!

Londres es la capital de Inglaterra y en Londres hay muchos sitios turísticos maravillosos. Hay palacios, galerías, estatuas estupendas, museos y restaurantes, teatros, conciertos de música clásica y moderna, cines, cafés, parques, y hoteles lujosos. Mis sitios favoritos son el museo de las ciencias y el zoo, donde hay animales exóticos de todas partes del planeta, incluso elefantes, serpientes y pingüinos. Los turistas visitan Londres para admirar la arquitectura y estudiar la cultura inglesa. La historia de Inglaterra es extremadamente interesante. El único problema en Londres es el tráfico que causa la contaminación del aire, y es un problema no solo regional. Es un problema global. Necesitamos soluciones para resolver los problemas. La primera solución es usar el transporte publico. En Londres los autobuses rojos son famosos y las bicicletas municipales son fenomenales.

London is the capital of England and in London there are many marvellous tourist sights. There are palaces, galleries, amazing statues, museums and restaurants, theatres, classical and modern music concerts and luxurious hotels are luxurious. My favourite places are the science museum and the zoo, where there are exotic animals from all over the world including elephants, snakes and penguins. Tourists visit London to admire the architecture and study English culture. The history of England is extremely interesting. The only problem in London is the traffic which causes air pollution, and it is is not just a local problem. It is a global problem. The first solution is to use the public transport and in London the red buses are famous and the municipal bicycles are fantastic.

Now turn over for the first vocabulary list…

NOTES

RELATIONSHIPS AND DESCRIBING PEOPLE

Family

en mi familia	in my family
mi padre	my father
mi madre	my mother
mis padres	my parents
mi hermano	my brother
mi hermana	my sister
mayor / menor	older/younger
soy hijo único	I'm an only child *(unique)*
mis abuelos	my grandparents
mi primo / mi prima	my cousin
mi tío	my uncle *(go for tea oh?)*
mi tía	my aunt
gemelos, gemelas	twins
el hijo	son
la hija	daughter
el bebe	baby
el marido	husband *(married-o)*
la mujer / esposa	wife
el chico	boy
la chica	girl
mi hermano se llama	my brother is called
no tengo hermanos	I don't have any siblings

REMEMBER

se llama = *is called,*

que se llama = *who is called*

How you get on

nos llevamos bien	we get on well
muchas cosas en común	lots of things in common
nos gustan	we like (plural thing)
los mismos programas	the same programmes
discutimos	we argue
nos gusta	we like (singular thing)
la misma música	the same music
estar mimado	to be spoilt
no le gusta(n)	he / she doesn't like

Types of relationship and family

el número crece	the number is growing
cada vez más	more and more
buenas relaciones	good relations
una relación	a relationship
enamorarse de alguien	to fall in love
el amor	love
conocer a	to meet
se conocen	they meet
el novio / la novia	boyfriend / girlfriend
casarse con	to marry *(house yourself)*
estar casado	to be married
un vínculo	a bond
prometer	to promise
volver a casarse	to remarry
una pareja	a couple *(pair)*
embarazada	pregnant

fiel	faithful
juntos	together *(roads at junction)*
una cita	a date
un beso	a kiss
un abrazo	a hug
contar con	to rely on *(count on)*
estar divorciado /-a	to be divorced
estar separado /-a	to be separated
una familia monoparental	single parent family
estar preocupado	to be worried
discutir	to argue
llorar	to cry
echar de menos	to miss
la echo de menos	I miss her

Hay un montón de tipos de familia hoy en día y todos tienen su valor. El número de personas solteras crece y cada vez más niños viven con hermanastros. Lo importante es el amor y la estabilidad y que un niño pueda contar con su familia para todo.

There are loads of types of family nowadays and they all have their value. The number of single people is growing and more and more children live with half sisters and brothers. The important thing is love and stability and that a child can rely on his or her family for everything.

.

Adjectives to describe people

grande	big
pequeño /-a	small *(like a Pekinese dog)*
alto /-a	tall *(altitude)*
bajo /-a	short
simpático /-a	nice

antipático /-a	not nice
alegre	cheerful
triste	sad
hablador /-a	chatty
trabajador /-a	hardworking
terco /-a	stubborn
delgado /-a	thin (*delicate*)
gordo /-a	fat
interesante	interesting
aburrido /-a	boring
divertido-a	fun (*diverting*)
gracioso/-a	funny (*gracias for being funny*)
serio /-a	serious
valiente	brave (*valliant*)
fuerte	strong (*a fort is strong*)
débil	weak (*a debilitating illness*)
cariñoso /-a	kind
amistoso /-a	friendly (*from amigo*)
tacaño /- a	mean
travieso /-a	naughty
pesado /-a	annoying
guapo /-a	good looking
feo /-a	ugly
viejo /-a	old
joven	young
deportista	sporty
perezoso /-a	lazy
orgulloso /-a	proud

Some lovely cognates for descriptions

activo /-a

tímido /-a

modesto /-a

arrogante

ambicioso /-a

artístico /-a

agresivo /-a

prudente

creativo /-a

convencional

generoso /-a

desorganizado /-a

elegante

famoso /-a

fascinante

atlético /-a

contento /-a

culpable

imaginativo /-a

impulsivo /-a

intolerante

optimista

pesimista

popular

religioso /-a

reservado /-a

romántico /-a

sarcástico /-a

superficial

sociable

diplomático /-a

tradicional

inteligente

estúpido -/a

There are more than 34 – but this gives you an idea of how many words you know without knowing…

Qualifying your adjectives

siempre	always
a veces	sometimes
a menudo	often
muy	very
bastante	quite
un poco	a bit
más / menos…. que yo	more / less … than me

Hair adjectives – tengo el pelo

largo / corto	long / short
liso / rizado	straight / curly
rubio / marrón	blonde / brown

General appearance

leva gafas	he wears glasses
una barba	a beard *(like barbed wire)*
un bigote	a moustache *('e got a bigote)*

parezco a mi madre	I look like my mother
nos parecemos	we look like each other

Mi madre tiene el pelo rubio y los ojos marrones. Es muy inteligente, pero a veces un poco tímida, y menos extravertida que yo. Normalmente nos llevamos bien porque tenemos muchas cosas en común como el deporte, pero a veces discutimos cuando no quiere que salga con mis amigas en vez de hacer mis deberes.

My mother has blonde hair and brown eyes. She is very intelligent but sometimes a bit shy, and less outgoing than I am. Normally we get on well because we have a lot in common like sport, but sometimes we argue because she doesn't want me to go out with my friends instead of doing my homework.

Clothes and things you carry

una camisa	a shirt *(camisole)*
una camiseta	a t-shirt *(litte camisa)*
pantalones	trousers *(pants are long)*
vaqueros	jeans
un vestido	a dress *(long vest)*
una falda	a skirt *(folded pleats?)*
los guantes	gloves
calcetines	socks *(concertina down legs)*
un cinturón	a belt *(from cintura=waist)*
una corbata	tie *(bat things away with it)*
una chaqueta	a jacket
un gorro	woolly hat
gafas	glasses
un paraguas	umbrela *(para agua = for water)*
un jersey	a jumper
zapatos	shoes

zapatillas de deporte	trainers
un abrigo	an overcoat
un impermeable	a raincoat *(impermeable)*
un monedero	wallet *(your money der)*
una maleta	suitcase *(need a mallet to shut it)*
una bolsa	a bag
un reloj	a watch or clock

Describing clothes

rayado /-a	striped
a cuadros	checked *(quadrants)*
ajustado /-a	tight *(needs adjusting!)*
con puntitos	spotty *(punto = dot)*
de cuero	leather
de lana	woollen *(from a llama?)*
de seda	silk
de algodón	cotton *(coddon)*
la moda	fashion
la marca	the brand

Colours

rojo /-a	red
naranja	orange *(norange)*
amarillo /-a	yellow
azul	blue *(azure)*
marrón	brown
rosa	pink
gris	grey

blanco /-a	white
negro /-a	black
verde	green *(verdant)*
morado /-a	purple

NOTES

HOUSE, HOME AND ROUTINE

una casa	a house
un piso / un apartamento	a flat
la planta baja	the ground floor
el primer / segundo piso	the first / second floor

Rooms

la habitación	room *(you inhabit it)*
el dormitorio	bedroom *(dormitory)*
la cocina	kitchen
el jardín	garden
el salón	lounge *(saloon)*
el garaje	garage
el vestíbulo	hall
el comedor	dining room *(from comer=to eat)*
el despacho	office *(send your dispatches)*

Structure

el edificio	building *(Eddy fixed it)*
la ventana	window *(for ventilation)*
la puerta	door *(port is a door to a country)*
las paredes	walls *(a pair of Eddy's)*
el tejado	roof
el techo	ceiling
la escalera	staircase *(escalator)*
la calefacción central	central heating

Furniture

los muebles	furniture
el armario	wardrobe *(for your armour)*
la cómoda	chest of drawers
la alfombra	rug
la cama	bed
la almohada	pillow
la estantería	bookshelf *('it stand here')*
el lavaplatos	dishwasher
la lavadora	washing machine
el grifo	tap *(grip it)*
el espejo	mirror *(looking 'especially' lovely)*
el horno	oven
el césped	lawn
el árbol	tree
la hierba	grass *(green herbs)*
las flores	flowers
detrás de	behind *(leave trash behind)*
delante de	in front of *(you leant on it)*
al lado de	next to *(a lad next to a lady)*
cerca de	near
compartir	to share *(into compartments)*
limpio	clean *(limp after all the cleaning)*
sucio	dirty
desordenado	untidy
los vecinos	neighbours *('they've seen us!')*

Household jobs

pasar la aspiradora	to do the hoovering

(think of somone passing the doorway with the aspirator – a machine that breathes in – respiration – all the dust)

poner la mesa	to lay the table
quitar la mesa	to clear the table
lavar los platos	to wash the dishes
preparar la comida	to do the cooking
arreglar mi dormitorio	to tidy my room
ayudar a mis padres	to help my parents
lavar el coche	to wash the car
limpiar la cocina	to clean the kitchen
hacer jardinería	to do the gardening
sacar la basura	to take out the rubbish *(in a sack)*
hacer de canguro	to do babysitting *(with baby in pouch)*
llenar el lavaplatos	to fill the dishwasher

Suelo arreglar mi dormitorio y limpiar la cocina y a veces paso la aspiradora, pero no lo hago todos los días porque los profes nos dan demasiados deberes.

I usually tidy my room and clean the kitchen and sometimes I do the hoovering, but I don't do it every day because the teachers give us too much homework.

NOTES

HOME AND ABROAD

la mejor región de…	the best region of
en mi barrio	in my area *(barriers protect)*
en la ciudad	in the city *(-dad ending = ity)*
en mi pueblo	in my village
mucho que hacer	a lot to do
vivo aquí desde hace	I have lived here for
ventajas	advantages

Places in the town

hay	there is / are
un lugar	place *(lug your stuff there)*
donde se puede	where you can
un cine	cinema
restaurantes	restaurants
polideportivos	sports centres
colegios	schools
un centro comercial	a shopping centre
mercados	markets
supermercados	supermarkets
iglesias	churches
parques	parks
almacenes	department stores
tiendas	shops
la acera	the pavement
la zona peatonal	the pedestrian zone

Things to do in town

ver películas	to see films
comer	to eat
ir de compras	to go shopping
hacer deporte	to do sport
salir por la noche	to go out at night
pasear al perro	to walk the dog
dar paseos	to go for walks
descansar	to rest / relax
encontrarse con amigos	to meet up with friends
tomar una copa	to have a drink
estudiar	to study
seguir viviendo aqui	to carry on living here
aprovechar	to make the most of

Town negatives

las desventajas	the disadvantages
lo que no me gusta	what I don't like
los atascos	traffic jams *(a task getting through)*
el tráfico	the traffic
la contaminación	the pollution
el ruido	the noise *(ruins it all)*
tirar basura	to drop litter
caro	expensive *(expensive car)*
la calle	the street
lleno	full

Shopping

ir de compras	to go shopping
abierto	open *(open 'a-beer-too'!)*
cerrado	closed *('there-are-no')*
dinero	money *(dinner money)*
el descuento	discount
hacer cola	to queue *(for coca cola)*
gastar	to spend *(on gas bill)*
malgastar	to waste *(bad spend)*
una tarjeta de crédito	a credit card
no puedo permitírmelo	I can't afford it

Countryside

mudarse	to move house
en el campo	in the countryside
hay menos ruido	there is less noise
tranquilo	quiet
vacio	empty *(vacant)*
espacios verdes	green spaces
aislado	isolated

Cuando sea mayor voy a seguir viviendo en la ciudad porque hay muchas cosas que hacer y para que pueda aprovechar la red de transporte. En el campo, aunque sea bonito, es demasiado tranquilo y aburrido.

When I'm older I'm going to carry on living in the city because there is a lot to do and so that I can make the most of the transport network. In the countryside, although it's pretty, it's too quiet and boring.

El transporte público

El transporte público	public transport
en autobús	by bus
en tren	by train
en coche	by car
en barco	by boat
en bici	by bike
en avión	by plane *(aviation)*
a pie	on foot
voy andando	I walk
caro	expensive *(expensive car)*
barato	cheap *(cheap bar)*
la estación de trenes	the train station
la parada de autobuses	the bus stop
rutas para ciclistas	cycle paths
una red de transporte	a transport network
tardo una hora en ir al...	it takes me an hour to get to...

Suelo ir al colegio en coche pero si hubiera más rutas para ciclistas iría en bici.

I usually go to school by car but if there were more cycle paths I would go by bike.

Holidays

ir de vacaciones	to go on holiday
reservar	reserve
una habitación	a room
fui a .... con	I went to.... with.....
pasar	to spend (time)
el vuelo	the flight

el viaje	the journey *(voyage)*
un billete de ida y vuelta	a return ticket
al extranjero	abroad *(strangers)*
durar	to last
perdí mi pasaporte	I lost my passport
perdí el avión	I missed the train *(lost it)*
el retraso	the delay
hacer las maletas	to pack the suitcases
el equipaje	the luggage
seguro /-a	sure
la seguridad	security *(-dad ending = ity)*
alojarse	to stay *(lodge yourself)*
el alojamiento	accommodation
un apartamento	a flat
un albergue	a hostel
un camping	a campsite
el hotel estaba	the hotel was situated
cerca de la playa	near the beach
la arena	the sand *(from sandy arenas)*
la entrada	entrance
la salida	exit / departure
los servicios / aseos	toilets
la vista	view
llegar	to arrive *(on your legs)*
había	there were / there was
sacar fotos	to take photos
probar	to try
los platos típicos	the local food

tomar el sol	to sunbathe
enviar cartas postales	to send postcards
comprar recuerdos	to buy souvenirs *(for the record)*
relajarse / descansar	to relax
divertirse	to have fun
conocer a gente nueva	to meet new people
salir a bailar	to go out dancing
me lo pasé bomba	I had a great time
tengo ganas de	I would like to
volver	to go back
en el future	in the future
esperar	to hope / wait for
esperar con ganas	to look forward to

Weather

hace sol	it's sunny
hace calor	it's hot
hace frio	it's cold
hace viento	it's windy
llueve	it's raining
hay tormentas	it is stormy
hay niebla	it's foggy
nieva	it's snowing
la lluvia	rain
las nubes	clouds

Festivals

las fiestas	festivals

el Año Nuevo	New Year
la Navidad	Christmas
el árbol de Navidad	Christmas tree
la boda	wedding
el nacimiento	birth
la Nochebuena	Christmas Eve
la Nochevieja	New Year's Eve
la Pascua	Easter
mandar	to send
postales de Navidad	Christmas cards
encender velas	to light candles
un desfile	a procession
dar / recibir	to give / receive
regalos	presents

NOTES

EDUCATION AND EMPLOYMENT

el mejor colegio	the best school
del mundo	in the world
lo que más me gusta	what I like most
los profes	the teachers
los alumnos	the pupils

Facilities

aulas	classrooms *(teacher = wise owl)*
laboratorios	laboratories
una biblioteca	a library
un comedor	a dining room
campos deportivos	sports fields
una piscina	a pool
el patio	the playground
donde se puede	where you can
jugar	to play
charlar	to chat
estudiar	to study

Hay una biblioteca donde paso mucho tiempo estudiando.

There's a library where I spend a lot of time studying.

Subjects

las matemáticas / ciencias   maths / sciences

la biología, la química, la física, música, geografía, historia

biology, chemistry, physics, music, geography, history

el francés, español, inglés, latín

French, Spanish, English, Latin

Mi asignatura favorita es el inglés porque es fácil y el profe es simpático, pero no me gustan las matemáticas porque el profe nos da demasiados deberes.

My favourite subject is English because it's easy and the teacher is nice but I don't like maths because the teacher gives us too much homework.

Education verbs

enseñar	to teach *(you need to be 'senior')*
aprender	to learn *(an apprentice learns)*
sacar buenas notas	to get good marks *(out of the sack)*
tener éxito	to succeed *(exciting!)*
revisar	to revise
pasar exámenes	to take exams
aprobar un examen	to pass an exam *(probably?)*
sacarse un reprobado	to fail *(reprobate!)*
preguntar	to ask
contestar	to answer *(in a contest)*
poner pruebas	to give tests

School day

al llegar	on arriving
las clases empiezan	lessons begin
la hora de comer	the lunch hour
el descanso	break time
el recreo	break time

School opinions

lo que más me gusta	what I like most

lo que no me gusta	what I don't like
tenemos que	we have to
llevar un uniforme	wear a uniform
los profes nos dan	the teachers give us
demasiados deberes	too much homework
las reglas son estrictas	the rules are strict
no se puede	you can't
comer chicle	to chew gum
usar el móvil	to use a mobile
llevar joyas	to wear jewellery
llevar maquillaje	to wear make-up

Plans for the future

seguir estudiando	to carry on studying
para que pueda	so that I can
conseguir un buen trabajo	get a good job
ayudar a la gente	to help people
ganar mucho dinero	to earn a lot
viajar por todas partes	travel everywhere
cambiar el mundo	change the world

Voy a seguir trabajando duro para que pueda conseguir un buen empleo. No sé exactamente lo que voy a hacer en el futuro. Lo importante es que sea interesante.

I am going to carry on working hard so I can get a good job. I don't know exactly what I'm going to do in the future. The important thing is that it is interesting.

Jobs

un empleo / un trabajo	job

azafata	air hostess
contable	accountant
abogado	lawyer
hombre de negocios	businessman
profesor /-a	teacher
científico /-a	scientist
peluquero /-a	hairdresser
periodista	journalist
enfermero /-a	nurse
marinero	sailor
escultor	sculptor
escritor	writer
pescador	fisherman
bombero	fireman
panadero	baker
matador	bullfighter
ingeniero /-a	engineer
cantante	singer
ama de casa	housewife

Cuando sea mayor voy a ser profe (note NOT UN PROFE) para que pueda aprovechar las vacaciones largas.

When I'm older I'm going to be a teacher so I can make the most of the long holidays.

SOCIAL ACTIVITIES AND HEALTH

la salud	health
malo / bueno para la salud	bad / good for you
sano / saludable	healthy
unos consejos	some advice
llevar una vida sana	to lead a healthy life
una dieta sana	a healthy diet
una dieta equilibrada	a balanced diet
la cantidad	quantity *(dad= ity)*
cinco porciones de	5 portions of
fruta y verduras	fruit and vegetables
deberíamos	we should
intentar	to try to
comer sano	eat healthily
evitar	avoid
la comida basura	junk food
el azúcar	sugar
la materia grasa	fat *(greasy)*
el alcohol	alcohol
tomar drogas	to take drugs
fumar	to smoke
hacer ejercicio	to do exercise
hacer deporte	to do sport
al aire libre	in the fresh air
dormir	to sleep
puede causar	it can cause
enfermedades graves	serious illnesses
el cáncer	cancer

la obesidad	obesity
se puede	you can
enfermarse	to get sick
engordar	to get fat
aunque sea malo	although it's bad
para la salud	for your health

Leisure

el ocio	leisure
en mi tiempo libre	in my free time
hago	I do
juego	I play
me gusta hacer	I like doing
me gusta jugar	I like playing

Sports that take hacer

deporte	sport
natación	swimming
equitación	horseriding
windsurf	windsurfing
vela	sailing *(turn the v over - sail)*
patinaje	skating *(pat the ice)*
gimnástico	gymnastics
ciclismo	cycling
piragüismo	canoeing
tiro con arco	archery
alpinismo	mountaineering
atletismo	athletics

jugar al ajedrez	to play chess
jugar al baloncesto	to play basketball
jugar al fútbol	to play football
jugar al hockey	to play hockey
jugar al cricket	to play cricket
un partido de fútbol	a football match
asistir	to attend
el jugador	player
el / la futbolista	footballer
el / la tenista	tennis player
el / la ciclista	cyclist
el / la atleta	athlete
el / la torero /-a / matador	bullfighter
el / la campeón /-a	champion
los espectadores	spectators
entrenarse	to train
recibir premios	to win prizes
el partido	match
el torneo	tournament
el balón	ball
el campeonato	championship
la carrera	race
en equipo	in a team

Other hobbies

periódicos	newspapers
libros	books
el ocio	leisure

leer	to read
revistas	magazines *(reveiws)*
novelas	novels
tebeos	comics
la lectura	reading
dibujar	to draw
pintar	to paint
dar paseos	to go for walks
ir de compras	to go shopping
escuchar música	to listen to music
ver la tele	to watch TV
tocar el piano	to play piano *(toc toc toc)*
cantar	to sing *(chant)*
bailar	to dance *(ballet)*
coleccionar	to collect
pescar	to fish
chatear en línea	to chat online

Me gusta pasar tiempo chateando en línea, en las redes sociales, enviando mensajes

I like to spend time online chatting on social networks, sending messages

Cinema and TV

ir al cine	to go to the cinema
ver la tele	to watch TV
una película	a film *(about pelicans?)*
mi pelicula favorita	my favourite film
mi programa favorito	my favourite programme
el canal	channel

telenovelas	soaps
telebasura	rubbish TV
documentales	documentaries
las noticias	the news *(notices)*
educativa	educational
una herramienta	a tool *(hairy-men tools)*
acabo de ver	I have just seen
una película de horror	horror film
una película de ciencia ficción	sci fi film
una película de guerra	war film
una película policiaca	detective film
una película del oeste	western
una película de amor	romantic film
una película de aventuras	adventure film
dibujos animados	cartoons
trata de	it's about
efectos especiales	special effects

Illness

hay el riesgo de	there is the risk of
una enfermedad	an illness
estar mal	to be unwell
sentirse	to feel
toser	to cough
el tos	cough
vomitar	to vomit
estar constipado	to have a cold
un resfriado	a cold

el sida	AIDS
el dolor	pain
una picadura	a bite / sting
la gripe	flu
ir al medico	to go to the doctor
pastillas	pills
medicina	medicine
medicamentos	medicine

Accidents

un accidente	an accident
tuvo un accidente	he had an accident
el incendio	a fire
apagar el incendio	to put out a fire
el humo	the smoke
la inundación	the flood
el peligro	the danger
un pinchazo	a puncture
tuve un pinchazo	I had a puncture
el testigo	the witness
el riesgo	the risk
sangre	blood
una multa	a fine
ayudar	to help
salvar	to save
gritar	to shout
chocar / pegar / golpear	to hit
atropellar	to run over

ocurir / suceder	to happen
ahogarse	to drown
el herido	the injured person
la herida	the injury
en la cárcel	in prison

Body parts

el brazo	arm
la mano	hand *(the main thing you need)*
el dedo	finger *(goes dead if you sit on it)*
el pie	foot
la pierna	leg *(longer than el pie)*
la rodilla	knee
la espalda	back
la cara	face
la oreja / el oído	ear
la cabeza	head *(cabbage)*
la nariz	nose
el estómago	stomach
el pelo	hair
los labios	lips
el diente / la muela	tooth
la voz	voice
los ojos	eyes
los hombros	shoulders
	(hombres - men have big shoulders)
la boca	mouth
	(for your bocadillo = sandwich)

Food and drink

comer	to eat
desayunar	to have breakfast
desayuno tostadas	I have toast for breakfast
almorzar	to have lunch
el almuerzo	lunch
cenar	to have dinner
la cena	dinner
la merienda	tea
pedir	to ask for
probar	to try
la cocina	cooking / the kitchen
cocinar	to cook
fresco	fresh

General food

pan	bread
tostadas	toast
cereales	cereal
mantequilla	butter *(meant-to-kill-ya)*
mermelada	jam
bocadillos	sandwiches
el arroz	rice

la carne	**meat**
el pollo	chicken
un bistec	a steak
la carne de vaca	beef *(meat of cow)*

el cerdo	pig / pork
el cordero	lamb
una chuleta	a chop
el jamón	ham
la ternera	veal
pescado	fish
las verduras	vegetables
las judías verdes	green beans
el pimiento	pepper
los guisantes	peas
la ensalada	salad
los champiñones	mushrooms (*champions)*
la lechuga	lettuce
el tomate	tomato
las zanahorias	carrots *(*bigger *than-your-ears)*
las espinacas	spinach
el esparrago	asparagus
la coliflor	cauliflower
las patatas	potatoes
las patatas fritas	chips
el pepino	cucumber
las cebollas	onions *(they-boil-ya)*
las frutas	fruit
la naranja	orange
las uvas	grapes
la cereza	cherry

el limón	lemon
las manzanas	apples *(man has Adam's Apple)*
el plátano	banana *(curls around a plate)*
el melocotón	peach *(peach skin feels cottony)*
pera	pear
la pina	pineapple
el albaricoque	apricot
el helado	ice cream
caramelos	sweets
pasteles	cakes

Las bebidas	drinks
una cerveza	beer
la leche	milk
un té	tea
un café	coffee
un vino tinto	red wine
un vino blanco	white wine
el agua	water
zumo	juice
el hielo	ice

en el restaurante

los platos	plates
el tenedor	fork
la cuchara	spoon
el cuchillo	knife
el vaso	a glass

el camarero	waiter
la cuenta	the bill
la propina	the tip

NOTES

MODERN WORLD AND ENVIRONMENT

el medioambiente	environment
los coches emiten	cars emit
gases tóxicos	toxic gases
las fabricas	factories
suben	rise up
en la atmosfera	into the atmosphere
la contaminación del aire	air pollution
el calentamiento global	global warming
el efecto invernadero	the greenhouse effect
los mares suben	the sea levels are rising
en peligro	in danger
el problema	the problem
va empeorando	is getting worse
amenazar	to threaten *(menace)*
los vertidos nucleares	nuclear waste
deberíamos	we should
se debe / hay que	it is necessary to
salvar	to save
proteger	to protect
mejorar	to improve
actuar	to act
los recursos naturales	natural resources
agotarse	to run out

Lo que más me preocupa es la contaminación del aire en las ciudades. Deberíamos usar el transporte público. Además, si hubiera más rutas para ciclistas podríamos ir en bici en vez de en coche. Cuando sea mayor, voy a seguir protegiendo el medioambiente para que los recursos naturales no se agoten.

What worries me most is air pollution in the cities. We should use public transport. Also, if there were more cycle paths we could go by bike instead of by car. When I'm older I'm going to carry on protecting the environment so that natural resources don't run out.

What do you for the environment?

ducharse – me ducho	to shower
para ahorrar agua	to save water
apagar las luces - apago	to turn off the lights
para ahorrar electricidad	to save electricity
reciclar - reciclo	to recycle
el cartón	cardboard
el vidrio y el plastico	glass and plastic
usar - uso	to use
el transporte público	public transport
ir en bici / hacer ciclismo	to cycle
comprar productos ecológicos	buy green products

Social problems

los sin techo	the homeless *(without a roof)*
dormir al raso	to sleep rough
duermen	they sleep *(radical changing)*
la pobreza	poverty
el mendigo	beggar *(clothes need mending)*
la inmigración	immigration

los inmigrantes	immigrants
los refugiados	refugees
la falta de dinero	lack of money *(it's a fault)*
la falta de casas	lack of houses
sin familias	without families
el paro	unemployment
las drogas	drugs
drogas blandas	soft drugs
piensan que es guay	they think it's cool
a largo plazo	in the long term
las cifras dan miedo	the figures are alarming

La publicidad — publicity

los anuncios	adverts
las medias	the media
la responsabilidad	responsibility
animar a…. a	to encourage …. to
quieren ser	they want to be
más delgado	thinner
influidos por	influenced by
por todas partes	everywhere
una mala influencia	a bad influence
por muchas razones	for many reasons
nocivo	harmful
informativo	informative
poderoso	powerful
lanzar una campaña	to launch a campaign
piensan que necesitan	they think they need

crear la avidez	create greed

Technology

la tecnología	technology
soy adicto	I'm addicted
no puedo prescindir de	I can't do without
el móvil	the mobile phone
el ordenador	the computer
enviar mensajes	to send messages
ponerse al día	to get up to date
navegar el internet	to surf the internet
descargar	to download
películas y música	films and music
las redes sociales	social networks
una página web	a website
ponerse en contacto con	to get in touch with
buscar información	to look up information
la intimidación	bullying
desconocidos	strangers
problemas de vista	eyesight problems
pegado a la pantalla	glued to the screen
perder amigos	to lose friends
volverse solitario	to get lonely
volverse triste	to get depressed
causar accidentes	to cause accidents

No puedo prescindir de mi móvil. Acabo de recibirlo para mi cumpleaños y lo uso para todo, para enviar mensajes, para descargar música y películas y para buscar información. Lo malo es que hay muchos peligros también. Se puede hablar con desconocidos en las redes sociales sin saber quiénes son. Uno puede volverse solitario y perder amigos, pasando todo el día pegado a la pantalla.

I can't do without my mobile. I just received it for my birthday and I use it for everything – to send messages, to download music and films and to look up information. The bad thing is that there are lots of dangers as well. You can talk to strangers on social networks without knowing who they are. One can get lonely and lose friends by spending all day glued to the screen.

NOTES

TIME AND PLACE

son las dos y media	it's 2.30
son las ocho y cuarto	it's 8.15
son las tres menos cuarto	it's 2.45
es la una menos diez	it's 12.50
a las dos	at 2
hoy	today
ayer	yesterday
mañana	tomorrow
la semana pasada	last week
la semana que viene	next week
el año pasado	last year
el año que viene	next year
el fin de semana pasado	last weekend
el fin de semana que viene	next weekend
a veces	sometimes
a menudo	often
siempre	always
nunca	never
normalmente	normally
cuando sea mayor	when I'm older
cuando era joven	when I was young

Days

lunes	Monday
martes	Tuesday
miércoles	Wednesday
jueves	Thursday

viernes	Friday
sábado	Saturday
domingo	Sunday

Months

enero	January
febrero	February
marzo	March
abril	April
mayo	May
junio	June
julio	July
agosto	August
septiembre	September
octubre	October
noviembre	November
diciembre	December

Mi cumpleaños es el nueve de mayo.   My birthday is 9 May.

COUNTRIES AND NATIONALITIES

Austria	Austria
Belgium	Bélgica
Denmark	Dinamarca
England	Inglaterra
France	Francia
Germany	Alemania
Great Britain	Gran Bretaña
Greece	Grecia

Holland	Holanda
Ireland	Irlanda
Italy	Italia
Netherlands	Paises bajos (m pl)
Russia	Rusia
Scotland	Escocia
Spain	España
Sweden	Suecia
Switzerland	Suiza
United Kingdom	Reino Unido
United States	Estados Unidos
Wales	País de Gales

Continents

Africa	África
Asia	Asia
Australia	Australia
Europe	Europa
North America	América del Norte
South America	América del Sur

Nationalities

American	americano/a
Austrian	austriáco /a
Belgian	belga
British	británico/a
Dutch	holandés/a
English	inglés/a

European	europeo/a
French	francés/a
German	alemán/a
Greek	griego/a
Irish	irlandés/a
Italian	italiano/a
Russian	ruso/a
Scottish	escocés/a
Spanish	español/a
Swedish	sueco/a
Swiss	suizo/a
Welsh	galés/a

PHRASES FOR THE ORAL EXAM

Positive opinions

vale la pena	it's worth it
me pone feliz	it makes me happy
me hace reir	it makes me laugh
tengo ganas de	I feel like
ir de vacaciones	to go on holiday
espero con ganas	I'm looking forward to
tengo suerte	I am lucky
lo que más me gusta es que	what I like most is
tengo buenas notas	I get good marks
me lo pasé bomba	I had a great time
no puedo prescindir de	I can't manage without
¡Qué bueno!	How brilliant!
el mejor país	the best country

Negative opinions

Lo que no me gusta es que	what I don't like is
Lo que más me preocupa es	what worries me most is
Estoy harto	I'm sick of it
¡Qué pesadilla!	What a nightmare
¡Qué horror!	How horrible!

Tengo expressions

Tengo suerte	I'm lucky
Tengo ganas de	I feel like
Tengo frio / calor	I'm cold / hot
Tengo que	I have to

Tengo hambre / sed	I'm hungry / thirsty
Tengo quince años	I'm 15
Tengo razón	I'm right
Tengo miedo	I am afraid
Tengo prisa	I'm in a hurry

Subjunctive expressions

Si tuviera mucho dinero	If I had a lot of money
Si fuera rico	If I was rich
Si hubiera	If there were
Si hubiera tenido el tiempo	If I had had the time
para que pueda	so that I can
aunque sea	although it is
no pienso que sea	I don't think it is
¡Ojalá pudiera!	If only I could

Pronouns attached to the infinitive or gerund

No puedo permitírmelo	I can't afford it
aprovecharlo	to make the most of it
Me gustaría verlo	I would like to see him

Spanish idioms

Estoy fastidiado	I'm not feeling well
Tengo el pie fastidiado	I've hurt my foot
¡Estoy machacado / agotado!	I'm exhausted!
He currado un montón	I've worked really hard
Voy a pegarme un madrugón	I'm going to get up early
madrugador	an early riser

Llueve a mares	It's pouring with rain
Cuesta un ojo de la cara	It costs an arm and a leg
Se me hace agua la boca	it makes my mouth water
Tiene un humor de perros	She is in a bad mood
Gastarse un riñón	to pay through the nose
Harina de otro costal	another thing entirely
ormir como un tronco	to sleep like a log

Words in common use

alguien	someone
algo	something
alguna parte	somewhere
algunos estudiantes	some students
ningún (-a)	no
ya	already
aun / incluso	even
lo mismo / la misma	the same
yo mismo / misma	myself
me da igual	I don't mind
no me importa	I don't mind
sin	without

Using haber

hay	there is
había	there was
habrá	there will be
habría	there would be
si hubiera	if there was

Using ser

es	it is
era / fue	it was
será	It will be
sería	it would be
si fuera	if it was / if I was

Expressing obligation and possibility

Hay que	it is necessary
Se debe	it is necessary
Deberíamos	we should
Se puede	you can
Podríamos	we could

Other publications also available on Amazon:

How to Ace your French oral

How to Ace your Spanish oral

How to Ace your German oral

French vocabulary for GCSE

The Common Entrance French Handbook

Brush up your French – a revision guide for grown-ups

The Advanced French Handbook

Ten Magic tricks with French

Spanish in a week

If you have any comments or questions on any of the content of this book, please do get in touch via my website

www.lucymartintuition.co.uk

Find me on Facebook and like my page to be first in the running for news and offers and free books!

And for some extra tips on how to impress examiners with your oral and writing, subscribe to my Lucy Martin Tuition YouTube channel.

Printed in Great Britain
by Amazon